BLINDED BY BENNY

BLINDED BY BENNY

BY

EVANGELIST GREG LOCKE

Post Office Box 1099 • Murfreesboro, Tennessee 37133

ISBN 0-87398-094-8

Printed and Bound in the United States of America

Contents

PREFACE

As I travel the world as a full-time, local-church evangelist, I am often confronted by people of certain denominational persuasions who are consumed with televangelism. While not all TV preachers are spreading falsehood and deception, there are many who certainly are. That is the case with Benny Hinn. He has been a careful study of mine for several years.

The Bible says that because of these false prophets "the way of truth shall be evil spoken of" (II Pet. 2:2). That is exactly what this man and many others like him have done. They have caused true and faithful preachers of the Gospel to come under unfair scrutiny and ridicule.

Mr. Hinn has accomplished what dozens before him have failed to do. He has built for himself an empire of followers worldwide and a multimillion-dollar business, and of course it is *all in the name of God*. He has rapidly become one of the most watched, heard and sought after televangelists in history.

Personal Freedom Outreach, which has followed this unusual ministry for several years, reports: "False prophecies, heretical doctrines, spurious healings, an exorbitant lifestyle and fabricated personal historical accounts have not been able to dethrone Hinn as the leading guru of Charismatics." Why is this? What is it about this man that causes so many people to be led astray? These are the questions that will be addressed in this booklet.

Putting this research into print will no doubt bring me under the attack of those who have been placed under his deceptive spell. However, it has been my personal burden for some time now to place in the hands of those who wish to know the truth a simple and concise work that accurately documents the "ministry" of Benny Hinn in his own words. Whenever a quote appears in bold print, it is a direct quote from Benny Hinn himself.

It is my prayer that you will read this book with an open mind and an open Bible. As Jesus said, "Ye shall know the truth, and the truth shall make you free" (John 8:32).

1

EXPOSING FALSE PROPHETS

Throughout history, people have always been interested in something new. Every decade or so, a new spokesman emerges and proclaims to have received "new revelation" from God. Naturally, people flock to hear what is going to be said. This has been the case now for quite a number of years with the "ministry" of Benny Hinn.

Mr. Hinn is an overwhelmingly charismatic personality that can razzle and dazzle a congregation with his delivery. There is little doubt that he has established a name throughout most of the world. Through his daily television program, *This Is Your Day,* his so-called healing crusades and his frequent appearances on the Trinity Broadcasting Network, he has made for himself a very notable name and a very wealthy living.

It is amazing to see the masses of people that follow this man's teachings. He has contradicted himself on countless occasions, and his false prophecies have failed miserably many times. Yet the crowds keep coming, and the offering buckets keep filling up.

We as God's people have a biblical obligation to expose those who "walk contrary" (Lev. 26:21) to the doctrines of the Word of God. We are also called to remove the spiritual blinders and unashamedly denounce false prophets (Matt. 7:15–23). However, there is also a more personal reason that I write these pages. I have received countless attacks and warnings that I should never speak against "God's man." Numerous people in my revival campaigns have been frustrated and oftentimes angry that I would dare to even mention this man's name in a derogatory manner.

A couple of years ago, my secretary called me and told me of a letter that I had received from a preacher in Tennessee. He had heard me speak for three nights at the Tennessee Statewide A. C. E. Student Convention in Murfreesboro, Tennessee. On Tuesday night, while preaching a message on Hell entitled "What's Everybody Screaming About?", I made several statements that reflected Benny Hinn's fallacies. The letter was an open rebuke to me for daring to speak against this marvelous man. (I will remind you that this was a preacher writing to me. He was cordial for the most part, but certainly worked at getting his point across.)

He told me that God was going to "remove his anointing from me" because I had spoken against Mr. Hinn. He used the verse "Touch not mine anointed, and do my prophets no harm" (I Chron. 16:22).

The man who wrote me that letter had purchased the tape from that Tennessee meeting and was able to give the date of the message, the context of the message and the exact quotes that I had preached. He used that age-old argument, "Judge not, that ye be not judged."

To be quite honest, when I speak against hypocrisy and falsehood, I do not consider that to be judging. Rather, I consider that I'm reading what the Judge said.

Near the end of the two-page letter he said, "Brother Locke, if Mr. Hinn had been in the audience that evening, I wonder if you would have said those very same things." Well, first of all, it is a foolish assumption on his part that I would be too embarrassed to speak against this man simply because he happened to be in the congregation. Second, not only would I have said the very same things, but if you read your Bible you will find out that Jesus would have said the same things as well.

Jesus was always very clear in his denunciation of false practices.

A study of the earthly ministry of the Lord Jesus Christ reveals that there is only one major group of people that gave him trouble. The drunkards, the fornicators, the cripples, the demon-possessed, the blind and the poor never once gave Jesus an ounce of trouble. As a matter of fact, they openly welcomed him into their communities. However, it was always that "religious" crowd that cared more about the traditions of men than the doctrines of the Word of God. The Bible names the Scribes, the Pharisees and the Sadducees. Jesus was always very clear in his denunciation of their false practices.

An interesting thing about Jesus' preaching is that he often waited for that particular group to show up before he began to expose them. He wanted the people to know about their crooked and deceptive ways. It is a sad day when even so-called preachers of the Gospel stand up to defend a man that has been proven time and again to be a false prophet.

You can decide for yourself. We are going to provide a lot of documentation about Benny Hinn, and then you as the reader may draw your own conclusions. Please understand, this small work is merely the tip of the iceberg in regards to our subject at hand. There are some great books that have been written on the subject. There are many, many articles, both for and against Benny Hinn, on the Internet. God said, "My people are destroyed for lack of knowledge" (Hos. 4:6). Study this issue, and then come up with your own conclusions and observations.

2

WHO IS BENNY HINN?

Benny Hinn was born in Israel and later raised in Canada. He has modeled his entire ministry after the false prophetess Kathryn Kuhlman. His unique stories and complete infatuation with Kuhlman are rather interesting and are sometimes reminiscent of the demonic. Mr. Hinn claims to have received his anointing from this legendary lady of lies.

Hinn's books and sermons are a continual reminder of his admiration for Kuhlman. We are going to use many of his own quotes, exactly as he said them. Many of these quotes are lengthy and very elementary in their word structure. Some sentences are completely non-understandable, but will most assuredly serve the purpose to show him untrue.

During his *This Is Your Day* television program on June 11, 1997, he told of a supposed vision that he had concerning his hero.

> **Ladies and gentlemen, I'm going to tell you something right now. The Lord showed me a vision about—goodness it's almost been a year now. And I—I—I—I can tell you**

I sense now the time has come when this vision is gonna be fulfilled. I had a vision of the night. What I saw, myself walk into a room. I've shared this before but just in case you—you've not heard it, I want you to hear it. I saw myself walk into room, and there stood Kathryn Kuhlman. And I've not seen Kathryn in a dream or a vision in years. Uh, when she died, the day she died, the morning she died, I had a dream what I—what I saw in a—in a—in a—in a casket with a white dress. And when I woke up in—in the morning, I knew she had died, and it was on the news that same morning. And so it's been many years. And there she was standing in this room, and she said to me—of course this was a dream, but really more of a vision. A lot of times dreams are really visions of the night, and the Bible calls them that when—when God gives to you in the fashion it really came with me. When I was a little boy, I saw the Lord in this dream. It was really so real. It was really a vision because when—when He appeared to me my body became electric just like electricity went through me, and when I awoke that electricity was still in my body. Well, anyway, in this one, in the vision that—that I saw—saw Miss Kuhlman. And she said, "Follow me." That's all she said. And I followed her to a second room. In that second room stood the Lord. When the Lord, uh—when—when I saw the Lord,

Kathryn disappeared. She was gone. And now the Lord looked at me and said, "Follow Me." And I followed Him to a third room. In the third room sat a gentleman—I still remember his face. I can tell you, I still remember the man's face. And the man sat in this wheelchair in that third room. There was a big hole in his neck. A tube down his throat. He was crippled on that wheelchair. And he had tubes down his body. Totally crippled, totally para—totally, of course, paralyzed. The Lord laid his hands on this man, and as he did the tube disappeared, the hole closed; he was completely healed and got up off the wheelchair. It was a creative miracle. Now I'm standing watching the Lord in this vision heal this man. And now as the man was healed, the Lord looked at me with piercing eyes—I'll not forget that one I'll tell you. Looked at me with piercing eyes and said, "Do it!" And the—and the dream and the vision came to an end.

That is probably the most confusing fairy tale I have ever read in my life. And if that is not bad enough, he then goes on to give a self-interpretation of what this "vision" really means.

When I woke, when I got up, when I came out of the vision, I was trembling and perspiring from head to toes. I know exactly what that vision means. It was Kathryn

Kuhlman who took me, who introduced me to the Holy Spirit. That is the meaning of that first room when she said, "Follow me." But when Kathryn was gone, Jesus was there. Kathryn did her job and was gone, and the Lord said, "Follow Me" into a third room. And there was this man. I believe I'm about to enter that third room. [Audience applause.] **I'm telling you I feel it. I sense it. I believe that room speaks of a dimension, a new dimension of the Spirit. I believe I've been in the second room now for the last seven years. What is amazing to me—what's amazing to me is God works or has worked in my life in seven-year cycles. I'm now in the seventh year—beginning the eighth of the ministry of these crusades. 1990 we started—March. This is what? '97. And just now I feel another platform, another dimension, another level is really coming. Well, saints, you're going to be a part of it. God—God has sent you as partners to be a part of it. So how many are ready to see greater things for the glory of God?**

Hinn has repeatedly referred to a "new dimension." Ecclesiastes tells us that "there is no new thing under the sun," so such unscriptural claims must be false. He has tried to give some kind of life to his visions by making them biblical. He has deceived them into actually believing that his ministry is one that is in touch with God and this marvelous "new dimension." I would not have believed that before I got saved, and I certainly will not believe it now that I am.

However, let's get back to his obsession with Miss Kuhlman. From the very beginning of his rising ministry, he has always attributed his success to the anointing that he received by Kuhlman. He has repeatedly stated that her grave carries a special anointing. He has also made the same foolish comments about the grave of Aimee Semple McPherson. Please note: McPherson was a hyperactive, twice-divorced "evangelist" who reportedly died of suicide. I am not in the least bit interested in that type of wonderful anointing.

From the beginning of his ministry, Hinn has always attributed his success to the anointing that he received by Kuhlman.

On April 7, 1991, at his former church, the Orlando Christian Fellowship, Benny Hinn delivered a sermon entitled "Double Portion Anointing." This was part three in a series called "Holy Ghost Invasion." In it, he makes some very scary statements that would lead one to question whether the "spirit" he is of is the Holy Spirit.

> **One of the strangest experiences I had a few years ago was Aimee's tomb in California. This Thursday I'm on TBN. On Friday I am gonna go and visit Kathryn**

> **Kuhlman's tomb. It's close by Aimee's in Forest Lawn Cemetery. I've been there once already, and every so often I like to go and pay my respects 'cause this great woman of God has touched my life. And that grave, uh, where she's buried, is closed. They built walls around it. You can't get in without a key, and I'm one of the very few people who can get in. But I'll never forget when I saw Aimee's tomb. It's incredibly dramatic. She was such a lady that her tomb has seven-foot angels bowing on each side of her tomb with a gold chain around it. As—as incredible as it is that someone would die with angels bowing on each side of her grave, I felt a terrific anointing when I was there. I actually—I—I—hear this, I trembled when I visited Aimee's tomb. I was shaking all over. God's power came all over me....I believe the anointing has lingered over Aimee's body. I know this may be shocking to you....And I'm going to take David and Kent and Sheryl this week. They're gonna come with me. You—you—you gonna feel the anointing at Aimee's tomb. It's incredible. And Kathryn's. It's amazing. I've heard of people healed when they visited that tomb. They were totally healed by God's power. You say, "What a crazy thing." Brother, there's things we'll never understand. Are you all hearing me?**

The Bible strongly condemns this type of foolishness. In Isaiah 65:2–4 we read, "I have spread out my hands all day unto a rebellious people, which walketh in a way that was not good, after their own thoughts; A people that provoketh me to anger continually to my face; that sacrificeth in gardens, and burneth incense upon altars of brick; *Which remain among the graves, and lodge in the monuments."*

The Jewish law taught that dead bodies were unclean, not something that held some type of mystical power in them. Numbers 19:11 states, "He that toucheth the dead body of any man shall be unclean seven days."

As you study the story in Mark 5 about the maniac of Gadara, the Bible says, "And always, night and day, he was in the mountains, *and in the tombs,* crying, and cutting himself with stones."

Now, someone may ask, "Are you saying that Benny Hinn is an occultist?" Look at the evidence and judge for yourself! These have been only a couple of quotes. If you study for yourself, you will find numerous quotes from Mr. Hinn about contact with dead people—especially Kathryn Kuhlman. He even wrote a book in 1999 entitled *Kathryn Kuhlman: Her Spiritual Legacy and Its Impact on My Life.*

As a matter of fact, Hinn's trademark of preaching in a white suit and gold jewelry can be attributed to the fact that Kathryn always spoke while wearing a flowing white garment trimmed in gold. It seems to me that he is more consumed with how Kathryn Kuhlman did things than he is in how God desires to do things.

There is an area of spiritism called necromancy in which people are supposed to receive communication from the dead. Benny Hinn openly admits to receiving revelations from dead people. Furthermore, he has experienced unusual and, in his own words, "unexplainable" power and ecstasy from the supposed saints of old. This type of nonsense is strictly forbidden in God's Word. Deuteronomy 18:10–12 says, "There shall not be found among you any one that maketh his son or his daughter to pass through the fire, or that useth divination, or an observer of times, or an enchanter, or a witch, Or a charmer, *or a consulter with familiar spirits,* or a wizard, *or a necromancer.* For all that do *these things* are an abomination unto the LORD."

That seems to be pretty plain teaching from the Bible. I am not by any means a supporter of other televangelists such as Jim Bakker and Jimmy Swaggart. However, for all of the moral failures that these men brought upon themselves, at least they were not so wicked as to try to bring the body of Christ into pagan spiritualistic practices.

3

A Deceiver!

It will not take very long to find more and more ridiculous prophecies that Mr. Hinn has stated in the past. His sermons are full of so-called revelations from the Spirit that have never come to pass. One of two things is true: *either God is lying to Benny Hinn, or Benny Hinn is lying to us*! Titus 1:2 says that "God...cannot lie," and Romans 3:4 adds, "Let God be true, but every man a liar."

Let us take a closer look at some of these heretical prophecies. On March 29, 2000, during a *This Is Your Day* television broadcast from the 700 Club Studios in Virginia Beach, Virginia, he stated the following:

> **I'm gonna show you the power of God upon young people. I know you may have seen this before, maybe you haven't—if you have, you'll get blessed all over again. I'm in Phoenix, Arizona this Thursday and Friday. What you're about to see is gonna happen there, so you in Phoenix make sure you show up for that crusade. Now, what you're**

gonna see happens usually at the last night at the end of the service for the young people. It's gonna be a powerful crusade—great, great things. Let me tell you something. The Holy Spirit has spoken. He told me He is about to show up. Oh, I got to tell you this just before we go. I had a word of prophesy from Ruth Heflin. You know who Ruth Heflin is? Ruth prophesied over me back in the '70s. Everything she said has happened. She just sent me a word through my wife and said the Lord spoke to her audibly and said that He is going to appear physically in one of our crusades in the next few months. Yes, she—I'm telling ya—she said the Lord spoke to her audibly and said, "Tell Benny I'm going to appear physically on the platform in his meetings." Lord, do it in Phoenix, Arizona in the name of Jesus! And in Kenya too, Lord, please! In fact, do it in every crusade. In Jesus' name.

My friend, this is absolute heresy! Furthermore, *it is a clear deception!* First of all, it never happened. He can claim he was quoting Ruth Heflin, but he passed it along as truth.

Second, it is not necessary to increase anyone's faith. "They that worship him must worship him in spirit and in truth" (John 4:24). We don't need a physical appearance of Christ to strengthen our faith. The Word of the living God is completely sufficient. Mark 13:21,22 says, "And then if any man shall say to you, Lo, here is Christ; or, lo, he is there; *believe him not: For false Christs and false prophets shall rise, and shall shew signs and wonders, to seduce, if it were possible, even the elect.*"

Hinn has claimed this kind of unscriptural nonsense for years, but he can certainly offer no proof of such erroneous claims. That was only one of many instances where this false prophet foretold a story of hocus-pocus.

The Word of the living God is completely sufficient.

In 1989, while still leading the congregation of the Orlando Christian Fellowship, he made some very interesting prophecies and attributed them to the Lord.

> **The Lord also tells me to tell you in the mid '90s—about '94 or '95, no later than that—God will destroy the community of America....He will destroy it with fire.**
>
> **The Spirit of God tells me—an earthquake will hit the East Coast of America and destroy much in the '90s.**
>
> **The Spirit tells me—Fidel Castro will die in the '90s...Holy Spirit just said to me, it'll be worse than any death you can imagine.**

Obviously, not one of these "prophecies" was fulfilled. So, that would make him a *false prophet* according to the Bible. Plain and simple!

After making these ridiculous comments to his

congregation and blaming them all on God, Hinn was said to have appeared "drunk in the spirit." When he finally came around, he made the statement, **"I would like to know what I said. I was totally gone."** This is not a scriptural sign of the filling of the Spirit.

Let us take another look at a false prophecy. During the spring 1999 Praise-A-Thon, Trinity's biannual fund-raiser, Mr. Hinn was brought in as a heavy hitter to raise the cash quickly. He knew full well of the hysteria and hype that Y2K was generating, and he took advantage of the situation. He went on to give a long, drawn out version of a dream that he had about the prophet Elijah. He worked diligently to establish his own credentials as a prophet. After speaking for a while on this subject, he said:

> **Pat Robertson, in January, said, "I have just come out of two days of prayer and fasting. The Lord has said to me that this year, 1999, would be the greatest year for the body of Christ, economically and spiritually, but beginning the year 2000, disasters would hit the world, economically and otherwise, and only those in the church who have been giving to God would be spared." So when I say to you here and in your home, "Increase your seed," God knows you can and you must because if you do not, you will be the one to suffer. And one final thing—if you break your promise, hear this! Some of you make a pledge and**

along the way you decide to forget about it. The Bible says that God will destroy the work of your hands if you do that. We can't play games with Him! Now, some of you will have to step out in faith tonight; you may not even have the money right now. In fact, most times you make a pledge you don't even have it. You know, you do not get under the kind of anointing I get under just because you sing hallelujah. There's a heavy price, and I would not want to be in the shoes of the one who touches the anointing. Don't touch the anointing! You know, if I was you and God spoke to me like this, I'd take it out of my investments to give to God now 'cause it's already spring and the year 2000 is almost next door.

Again, he can claim he was only quoting Robertson, but he used it as established truth, and that is a prime example of taking advantage of a situation. It is reported that the phone lines were completely jammed as viewers called in their pledges. The year 2000 has come and gone, but I can guarantee that the Trinity Broadcasting Network didn't give any of the money back.

All of God's people would do well to read Jeremiah 14:14: "Then the LORD said unto me, *The prophets prophesy lies in my name: I sent them not, neither have I commanded them, neither spake unto them: they prophesy unto you a false vision and divination, and a thing of nought, and the deceit of their heart.*"

In Jeremiah 23:16 we read, "Thus saith the LORD of hosts, Hearken not unto the words of the prophets that prophesy unto you: they make you vain: *they speak a vision of their own heart, and not out of the mouth of the LORD.*"

The boldest denunciation of these false prophets is found in Deuteronomy 18:20–22. "But the prophet, which shall presume to speak a word in my name, which I have not commanded him to speak, or that shall speak in the name of other gods, *even that prophet shall die.* And if thou say in thine heart, How shall we know the word which the LORD hath not spoken? When a prophet speaketh in the name of the LORD, *if the thing follow not, nor come to pass, that is the thing which the LORD hath not spoken, but the prophet hath spoken it presumptuously:* thou shalt not be afraid of him."

Benny Hinn has certainly been known to stretch the truth. On October 22, 1997, on his daily television show, he claimed that God had moved on his behalf and that the Florida Panthers hockey team had canceled a game in order for a Hinn Crusade to be held in the Miami Arena. He said:

> **The Lord spoke to me while in Miami, here the first day, and said, "Come back here for Good Friday." We were supposed to be somewhere else. And I said, "Lord, open the way." And guess what? The manager of the Miami Arena canceled the hockey game so we can have the arena on Good Friday,**

April 10, 1998. And I think that's marvelous, don't you?

Mr. Yves Brault contacted the special events department at the Miami Arena to ask them if this were really true. And, wouldn't you believe it, it was not. He was specifically told that "no hockey game was ever scheduled for the 10th." The game was scheduled for the 9th between the Panthers and the Philadelphia Flyers. The arena spokesperson said, "We can't cancel a game because the tenants take preference, and the Panthers are the tenants in our building. But, right after the hockey game, we'll start setting up for Benny Hinn." This is the kind of misrepresentation that characterizes Benny Hinn Ministries.

Other examples of this are his conflicting stories regarding his own personal salvation experience. He originally stated that his conversion was in 1972. However, this contradicts a taped testimony in 1987 in which he described an angel taking him into a room at a high school, and there he was saved. That is documented in his book *Good Morning, Holy Spirit*. In a written devotional from 1981, we read, **"I got saved in Israel in 1968."** Yet again during a St. Louis sermon in 1983, he says that he was witnessed to after moving to Ontario, Canada and was saved as a result of the witness. He tells of all his family members giving their hearts to the Lord on separate occasions. But in his book *War in the Heavenlies,* released in 1984, he tells that his family were all saved at the same time.

The following story is adapted from the book *The Confusing World of Benny Hinn.*

In May of 1983, Hinn and five others survived a plane crash. This was discussed on the *PTL* show with Paul and Jan Crouch. Hinn claimed the Lord spoke, saying, **"'Nothing will happen to you.' When I walked out of the plane, Paul, I did not have a scratch on my body."** Paul then responded, "We remember that! Not a scratch." Hinn claims that he walked away without a scratch or an injury and that right on the spot he healed another passenger's eye that came out of its socket. The documentation proves otherwise. Two newspaper reports, the FAA, the National Transportation Safety Board, the sheriff's department and the hospital all agree on a different account than Hinn's. The *Orlando Sentinel* reported that all six occupants were injured. The Avon Park paper reported that Hinn was in a state of shock and said, **"It will be the last time I ever fly in one of these** [single engine planes] **again."** There were no miracles reported by Benny Hinn, the newspaper or the victims. The records show that the Hinns were in the hospital. Benny was released after two days, but his wife remained hospitalized for three days. According to the sheriff's report, Benny had multiple contusions, abrasions and lacerations. The man whose eye was said to have been healed testified that Hinn prayed for his eye, but the right eye that was injured was not healed. After various operations, he is able to see today. This is attributed to surgery, not to Mr. Hinn laying hands on him.

4

RAISING THE DEAD?

The list could go on and on, and some of the reports are even more bizarre than those we have mentioned. There have been several broadcasts on his own program as well as on TBN that Mr. Hinn has boldly proclaimed to have raised the dead. Give me a break! If Benny Hinn could raise the dead, every funeral parlor in the world would be contacting him to make "house calls." This alleged miracle has *never* been verified. And the reports change nearly every time it is given. Interestingly enough, it happened overseas, where there is little to no English spoken and where no accountability can be attached to this preposterous claim.

While we are on the subject of ridiculous claims and the raising of the dead, notice the following conversation between Benny Hinn and Paul Crouch. On October 19, 1999, during a *Praise the Lord* program on the Trinity Broadcasting Network, Mr. Hinn said:

> **But here's first what I see for TBN. You're going to have people raised from the dead watching this network. You're going to have**

people raised from the dead watching TBN. Programs—just plain programs—programs that haven't done much when it comes to supernatural manifestations—teaching programs. It's not going to be a Benny Hinn saying, "Stretch out your hands." It's going to be your average teaching program, your normal Christian program that's blessing the church. There's going to be such power on these programs people will be raised from the dead worldwide. I'm telling you, I see this in the Spirit. It's going to be so awesome—Jesus, I give you praise for this—the people around the world—maybe not so much in America—people around the world who will lose loved ones, will say to undertakers, "Not yet. I want to take my dead loved one and place him in front of that TV set for twenty-four hours."

Paul Crouch then responded, "Benny Hinn! Jesus!" Mr. Hinn continued:

I'm telling you. People will be—people—I'm telling you, I feel the anointing talking here. People are going to be canceling funeral services and bringing their dead in their caskets, placing them—my God! I feel the anointing here—placing them before a television set, waiting for God's power to come through and touch them. And it's going to happen time and time—so much it's going to spread. You're going to hear it from Kenya to Mexico to Europe to South

America, where people will be raised from the—so much so that the word will spread that if some dead person be put in front of this TV screen, they will be raised from the dead, and they will be by the thousands. You wait....I see quite something amazing. I see rows of caskets lining up in front of this TV set, and as people are coming closer I see actually loved ones picking up the hands of the dead and letting them touch the screen and people are getting raised as their hands are touching that screen....With this program—I'm not talking about my program—I'm talking about programs, plain programs aired—the glory of God will be so on TBN that there's going to be divine resurrection happening as people bring their loved ones to the TV set.

The lack of discernment among so-called Christians is appalling.

Honestly, I must say that has to be the most immature and spiritually pathetic thing I have ever heard in my life. The lack of discernment among so-called Christians these days is appalling. Thousands have been deceived into believing this unbiblical nonsense. One thing is for sure: *if laying a Bible on a dead person cannot raise them, then a television set will certainly not do it!*

During the very same broadcast, Benny Hinn also

said, **"TBN will no longer be just a television network. It will be an extension of Heaven to earth."** Mr. Crouch responded by saying, "My Jesus, have mercy. Ohhhhh!" Then Benny goes on to say:

> **The Lord just said to me these words—I'm hearing myself say them for the first time—TBN will not be only a Christian network. It will be an extension of Heaven to the earth. An extension—it will be like a tube from Heaven that the earth can look and say, "I'm looking at Heaven; I'm partaking of Heaven. I'm getting connected to Heaven through this TV tube." If I can say it, it will be Heaven's signal to earth. It will be as though Heaven is transmitting and earth is receiving through that set. So if you want to go to Heaven, you want to see Heaven, you want to taste Heaven, turn on that channel, 'cause you will.**

5

THE CRUSADE HYPE

Another of Benny Hinn's bogus claims deals with his "health and wealth" prosperity message. In his book *Rise & Be Healed,* on page 14 he states:

> **Sickness does not belong to you. It has no part in the body of Christ. Sickness does not belong to any of us. The Bible declares if the Word of God is in our life, there will be health, there will be healing—divine health and healing. There will be no sickness for the saint of God. If Moses could live such a healthy life, so can you....He promises to heal all—everyone, any, any whatsoever, everything—all our diseases! That means not even a headache, sinus problem, not even a toothache—nothing! No sickness should ever come your way.**

This is certainly not the case with the great man Job. He lost his finances, his family, his flesh and his friends all in two chapters of the Bible. I suppose these prosperity preachers would tell us that he had a lack of faith. Well, God said he was the most faithful man in the whole land. Their wicked theology works only when they are healthy and while the money is flowing in by the handfuls. Hinn then later claimed that he once had a headache and that he turned his own television program on and was healed watching himself. It's easy to make up nice little stories when no one is around to see for themselves. It's kind of like quoting from someone who is dead. You can make a dead man say anything that you want him to.

One of the most controversial aspects of Hinn's ministry is the unusual way in which he conducts his crusades. The crowd is "hyped" up by continual singing. Hinn makes his audience wait and wait with eager anticipation. The people sing choruses many times over, and the auditorium is fixed with special lighting. All of this creates just the right mood. He *always* takes the stage as "How Great Thou Art" is being sung. He has some very unique tactics, to say the least. He is quite a showman, and he has a hypnotic effect on the crowd.

He throws the "Holy Spirit" around, using the third Person of the Trinity as his servant.

He repeatedly talks of people being "slain in the spirit." Again, he utilizes the same propaganda that Kathryn Kuhlman used in her "miracle crusades" many years ago. However, Hinn has a new flare about his approach. He, like Kuhlman, touches people's foreheads and necks. But Benny can "throw" his so-called anointing from a distance.

On November 24, 1991, Mike Thomas reported the following in *Florida Magazine:*

> Winded catchers try to keep up with the toppling bodies. He [Hinn] rears back and with a pitching motion slays the entire choir with one toss. **"That's power,"** yells Benny. **"POWER!"** Hinn takes off his custom-tailored jacket and rubs it briskly on his body. He is rubbing the power into the jacket. Then he starts swinging it wildly, like the biblical David swinging his sling. He decks his followers left and right. Bam! Bam! Bam! The stage vibrates with their landings. Then he throws it [the "anointed" jacket]. Another bam! As a catcher moves to pick up a woman, Hinn slays him....Then he slays the catcher who caught the catcher. When Benny Hinn is moved, nobody is safe from the power....He blows loudly into the microphone....Hundreds fall backward....A woman collapses in the aisle and begins to babble. And then, suddenly, Benny is gone. The power vanishes from the room, and the people stare in stunned silence.

This aspect alone of Hinn's meetings is enough to condemn him. He capriciously throws the Holy Spirit around in the most irreverent fashion, using the third Person of the Trinity as his servant to attract attention to himself. Hinn acts as though the "anointing" is some metaphysical power at his disposal, to be rubbed off onto objects. It looks impressive, works largely by the power of suggestion, but has no purpose except to make people stand in awe of him. "It's scary," says Bill James, a former church member. "The people are mesmerized.... When he comes out, he's like God."

It is interesting to note that Hinn claims over one thousand people are healed at each "Miracle Crusade." However, none of these are viable testimonies, and he is *using the very same trick that hypnotists and magicians have used for centuries.* You would think that naïve "Christians" would wake up and get some discernment. Jim Jones used the same kind of control over people with destructive results.

I know a lady in Severn, Maryland who is a member of the Chesapeake Baptist Church where her pastor is Dr. Barney Lyons. She has told me personally on several occasions a terrible story about Mr. Hinn.

She was a desk clerk at one of the nicest hotels in New York City, and Benny Hinn was scheduled to stay in the top floor suite of that hotel. When he arrived, she said he was "a very rude man." He went upstairs to see his suite and rejected it. He said that it was not nice enough. (My desk clerk friend reports that the room rented for well over $1,500 a night.)

As he came back downstairs, there was a lady in the lobby with a crippled son. This lady was in desperation. She had spent loads of money following Mr. Hinn through three different cities trying to get his attention. When he was told that she desired to see him, he said loudly and impatiently, "I don't have time for that right now."

I realize that people can get very busy with life. I also realize that pressures can mount up and frustration can follow. However, being frustrated about a $1,500 hotel room and turning away a crippled boy and his mother is uncalled for. Jesus said, "Suffer the little children to come unto me."

If Mr. Hinn had a monopoly on the Holy Spirit and could instantly heal people, *then he certainly would.* If God were to give that power to any man, then He would assuredly give him the wisdom and compassion to use it. Benny Hinn only heals people during his super-duper, overly charismatic stage show that he cloaks with the name "Miracle Crusade."

Even during the crusades, he has selective healing. I personally called the offices of Benny Hinn Ministries. I told them that my wife Melissa has asthma, and she does. I asked what I would have to do to get her on the platform for prayer. (By the way, I would not have taken her. I was merely testing the waters to get an answer.)

The lady said, "Sir, the only people who can get up on the platform and testify are those who have previously been healed in another crusade." I have watched with my own eyes, on the man's own program, as people got silenced in mid-sentence because they seemed to have slipped up and were about to say something they were not supposed to.

If you want answers, then call Hinn's ministry for yourself. The number is 1-817-722-2000. The ministry is based outside of Dallas, Texas.

6

WHAT HAPPENS TO THE MONEY?

Benny Hinn Ministries often looks more like a giant fund-raising organization. His TV programs, his Web site, his crusades—everything the man does has a heavy price tag attached to it.

Mr. Hinn has been dreaming for some time now of a fifty-acre theme park. In this park he desires to have a garden with life-size bronze statues depicting healing scenes from the Bible. *The Healing Gardens* will be the name. He has raised "boatloads" of money for it over the past several years. What the donations get you is interesting:

$150,000 will put your name on the cornerstone of the People's Cathedral.

$30,000 will do the very same thing, but it will be in the Hall of Faith.

$15,000 will get you remembered at the walls of the Healing Gardens.

$4,000 to $8,000 will get your name engraved on the Fountain of Healings.

$2,000 will get your name on a rock in the Healing Stream.

$1,500 will allow you to be remembered at the Eternal Flame of Healing.

$150 will hardly get you to the Prayer Tower.

The teaching of this ministry seems to be: The bigger the donation, the bigger the blessing from above. In the next several pages, I am going to give you the documentation by several reliable sources about Benny Hinn Ministries in regards to money.

On December 27, 2002, NBC aired a program on *DATELINE* about Mr. Hinn. *DATELINE* was able to get in with hidden cameras and give some very revealing interviews. It was well documented, and all sources were quoted in context after much study and hard work. What you are going to read for the next few pages will be excerpts of part 2 of the show entitled "Former Insiders Question What Happened to Some of the Church Money." As has been the case throughout the book, quotations in bold print are direct quotes from Benny Hinn.

> **"Only those who have been giving to God's work will be spared."** The money starts pouring in at Benny Hinn's crusades, thousands of people filling up hundreds of pastor Benny's collection buckets at every service we attended. Chris Hinn [Benny's brother] says, "One side cash, one side checks." A 1994 security tape shows Hinn staffers and volunteers counting the collection money at a crusade. Mike Estrella says that for three years in the mid-1990s he was one of those responsible for counting crusade collections in his capacity

as Benny Hinn's head usher. At that time, Estrella says, he was a devoted follower, and he still credits pastor Benny with curing his heart condition.

"In cash, what was the biggest night you counted?" asked Bob McKeown.

"In cash? Well, one night I counted $420,000," responded Mr. Estrella.

Steve Brock, one of the platform men, says to the audience, "A dollar a day. Everybody say it with me—a dollar a day."

It may sound like they start out small, but the numbers soon get very big. According to documents provided by the Trinity Foundation and published reports, Benny Hinn has more than 100,000 people who promise to give him a dollar a day. If they keep that pledge, that would add up to at least $3 million a month—$36 million a year. The people on the list seemed to be even more generous than that—it appears some of them pledged and gave more than $100,000 apiece last year.

"The greatest thing you can do for your finances is to give to the work of God." On TV, and at his crusades, Hinn promises that God will improve not only your health, but your financial life as well—perhaps by getting you out of debt with an unexpected financial windfall. But first, you have to give money to his ministry. Hinn calls it **"sowing the seed."**

"Amen. So expect a financial harvest, but you have to sow a seed to see it happen—you may want to call your seed in today. Our 800 number is on the screen."

And the money Benny Hinn's ministry gets is not only in the form of donations....In recent years, the Hinn Ministries total annual income has increased dramatically from $50 million in 1997 to the latest estimate—that the ministry says is inaccurate—of more than $100 million a year. *And because the ministry is registered as a church, all that money is tax-free and Benny Hinn is under no legal obligation to make his finances public.*

Paul Nelson is president of ECFA, the Evangelical Council for Financial Accountability. Billy Graham, Pat Robertson and the Salvation Army are among its thousand-plus members who voluntarily disclose to potential donors more financial information than the law requires. "We believe that most people would like to know that the charities they give to are governed responsibly, that they practice disclosure of their finances and other activities, that they willingly answer questions, and that they raise funds with integrity," says Nelson.

Members release audited financial statements, including the salaries of their ministers. Benny Hinn is not an ECFA member. He wouldn't tell us his annual salary, but five years ago [1998] he acknowledged it was between $500,000 and $1,000,000 a year. And Hinn won't specify how his ministry's money is spent, except to say he doesn't personally benefit from any of it.

For years, Michael Cohen and his wife were church members under Mr. Hinn. He also belonged to Hinn's security detail, traveling the world with him. Cohen recalls an incident after a service at the church where he says pastor Benny bragged about his financial conquests. "Like, one little grandmother one time came up and cried, I think she said, 'This is my last five dollars.' And we got back in the Green Room and he said, '**Ha! I got her last five dollars, guys.**'"

> *"Ha! I got her last five dollars, guys."*
> *—Benny Hinn*

The ministry says the incident never happened.

As for his lifestyle, pastor Hinn has explained that some of the perks he has enjoyed—like custom-made suits and expensive cars—have been paid for by his personal income, including royalties from his many books. While that may be true and legal, *it's only part of the story.* [My grandfather used to tell me that a half truth is a whole lie.]

According to Trinity Foundation, the biggest customer for pastor Benny's books is pastor Benny's own ministry. Trinity says the Hinn ministry buys thousands of the books for which Hinn apparently collects the royalties. The ministry then offers them for sale at crusades and on its Web site and gives them away to donors. According to Paul Nelson of ECFA, that kind of business is too close for comfort and wouldn't be allowed if Hinn belonged to his [Nelson's] organization.

The Hinn ministry also spends a great deal on pastor Benny's lifestyle while he's on the road. These records show hotel suites for well over a thousand dollars a night and transatlantic flights on the Concorde at more than $8,000 round trip—that is, before pastor Benny began flying in a multimillion-dollar private jet.

Benny Hinn's followers may not know how all of their donations are spent. For example, there's Hinn's palatial new home, now being built for $3.5 million in an exclusive, gated community overlooking the Pacific Ocean. The plans call for more than 6,000 square feet—7 bedrooms, 8 bathrooms and a basement garage with enough space for ten cars. Who's paying for that? Not pastor Benny. That mansion on the Pacific is considered the Hinn Ministries' church residence, or "parsonage," and the ministry is picking up all the expenses for the land, construction, even property taxes. The ministry says the house is a good investment, but Paul Nelson of ECFA says Benny Hinn should be concerned about the perception of that house deal. He says the expenditure of millions of dollars of church money on a house for its leader is almost unprecedented.

Cohen and Estrella [both aforementioned ex-members of Hinn's staff] maintain that they were true believers who put their faith in a man they thought could bring hope and healing to millions. "What I saw was a big business rolling millions of dollars every year, many people getting rich," says Mike Estrella, "and the rich getting richer, and the poor getting worse."

What you have been reading is the very script that appeared on NBC's *DATELINE*. I think that much of what has been said is quite an eye opener. Please don't misunderstand what I am trying to say. I believe that God's man [I use the term in a general sense and certainly not in reference to Mr. Hinn] should be well taken care of. I am not against nice clothes, a fancy car or even a big house. That doesn't bother me. What bothers me is *financial secrecy, misinformation, scandals and flat out greed.* The Bible says, "Love of money is the root of all evil." Benny Hinn is a man that passionately serves his god—*and that god is money*

Another secular news report was aired on CNN's *IMPACT* program on March 16, 1997. This program listed several documented facts about Hinn's ministry.

CNN reported that on one of Hinn's trips, his personal hotel bill was $2,200 a night.

One of Hinn's former bodyguards was tired of the dishonesty and was going to go public about the unaccountable money flow. He was paid $103,000 to remain quiet.

Benny Hinn Ministries receives between 15,000 and 18,000 pieces of mail every week. Scores of the envelopes are filled with donations. They have "forty people working forty shifts" just to handle and sort all of the mail.

Since 1995, Hinn's ministry intake has increased well over 50%.

One report said that Benny Hinn was overheard offering his autograph on a book for a $100 "donation."

These are not things that some Baptist preacher has "cooked up" in the pulpit. These are the things that unsaved media and viewers alike are saying. So much for a man of God being "above reproach."

7

Heretical Doctrines

The question may arise in someone's mind as to why I would even take the time to research and write a book on Benny Hinn's ministry. However, it must be realized that we are not dealing with a "Podunk," uneducated hillbilly. This man does not have a small group of ignorant followers. We are dealing with a multimillion-dollar industry that has deceived countless millions. This man is very shrewd in his dealings.

Here is yet another illustration of how many people actually believe in the miracle-working madness of this false prophet. On Sunday, April 30, 2000, four people died in Nairobi, Kenya, during one of Mr. Hinn's "Miracle Crusades." It was reported in the *Kenya Times.* These people were very seriously ill but had been released from the hospital in order to attend one of the meetings in hope of divine healing. Instead of being healed, they all died in the service. Ten other people were seriously injured after falling out of trees. They had climbed the trees in order to get a glimpse of the American preacher. Hinn's televised program is aired throughout Kenya, and he has a very large following there.

There is not a person in the world with a logical, thinking mind that will not agree that this man has created an empire of "faithful followers." It is believed by many that the man has misappropriated funds. His influence over much of the world is spellbinding, and his claims are radically exaggerated. But in the midst of all that we have brought to light during these pages, we have said nothing about the heretical doctrines that Mr. Hinn has been teaching for years.

Not being educated is no excuse for biblical ignorance.

Time would not allow for a thorough study of this particular aspect of his ministry. Other books, with much more information, have been written. However, we will deal with a few of these weird and unscriptural ideas.

Many of the ridiculous doctrines that he teaches are absolutely foolish in nature. It seems that he is always trying to come up with something new. After a while, the "old stuff" starts wearing out, and some sort of new theology is needed to impress people. It has been well said: "If it's new, it's not true; and if it's true, then it's not new."

Too many so-called preachers try to read into the Bible what is *not* there, and they try to read out of the Bible what *is* there. I will say this in his defense: Mr. Hinn has never had any formal training in the

Bible. He never attended any type of Bible school and has never been trained for the ministry. I certainly do not believe that everyone needs to go to a college, and I am by no means insinuating that he is a heretic *because* he never enrolled in a school. He has said himself, **"The Lord launched me into ministry almost overnight."** That doesn't bother me. There have been many men in the past who have never been educated, but they have been mightily used of God. However, these men were avid students of God's Word.

Benny Hinn seems to get off on a spiritual tangent in many areas of his doctrine. Not being educated is no excuse for biblical ignorance and poor exegesis. There are some things that he teaches that would be considered borderline. There are other things that he used to teach but has since changed his mind and his position on after receiving a lot of pressure from the critics.

For example, for many years he taught that there were *nine* in the Godhead. His theology was basically that the individual members of the Trinity—God the Father, God the Son and God the Holy Spirit—consisted of three persons *each*, making it a grand total of **"nine in one."**

Although he has since forgotten that ridiculous doctrine, he used to teach other bold and blatant heresies. He taught that when Jesus "became sin for us," He took upon Himself the nature of Satan himself and had to be "born again" in Hell. On December

1, 1990, during an interview on the Trinity Broadcasting Network, Hinn said the following:

> **He** [Jesus] **who is righteous by choice said, "The only way I can stop sin is by Me becoming it. I can't just stop it by letting it touch Me; I and it must become one." Hear this! He who is the nature of God became the nature of Satan where He became sin!**

That is not only an idiotic interpretation of Scripture, that is an ungodly and perverted assumption on Mr. Hinn's part.

Many of his early teachings are completely in line with New Age teachings. If you notice, he never makes any comments about the New Age Movement. As a matter of fact, if you study him closely, you will find that he is very much a part of it. He uses hypnosis, Eastern mysticism, transcendental meditation, channeling and a host of other "Harry Potter" tricks.

During the very same interview mentioned above, Hinn asserted that though we are not Almighty God Himself, nevertheless **"we are now divine."** Whatever happens to come to his mind as he reads the Bible, he seems to automatically ascribe it to **"revelation from God."** But that is not all. Hinn actually rewrote Job 1:21, changing "the LORD hath taketh away" to **"the Lord never taketh away."** If that is not enough, read the following list of blunders and outright heretical statements.

> **Never, ever, ever go to the Lord and say,**

"If it be thy will." Jesus made a mistake when He said that.

No Christian should ever be sick.

We Christians possess power in our mouths to heal or kill, just as witches possess it.

Christ would have sinned without the Holy Ghost and would have remained in the grave if the Holy Spirit had changed His mind about raising Him from the dead.

We are little gods and even part of God with all the power of God; and we are little messiahs, everything that Jesus ever was.

If you are really interested in what this man teaches, just borrow one of his many books from the library or watch a segment or two of his daily television program. Both are filled to overflowing with unbiblical, ludicrous and childish doctrines. One thing is for sure: if it is the Holy Spirit that is giving Benny Hinn all of these ideas and doctrines, then it is certainly in complete contradiction to what He, the Holy Spirit, has given us in the revelation of God's Word. We know that Almighty God is not a liar and will *never* contradict what He has previously said. Based upon that principle, we must logically conclude that someone is lying. *It is either Mr. Hinn or the Holy Spirit!* You can be the judge as to which one it actually is.

Even if the man preached the Gospel, which he

most certainly does not, he would still need to be discounted as a false prophet simply for his irreverent use of spiritual things.

Think just for a moment about how he hypes his audience. Thousands of people are eagerly anticipating a word from the Lord and a mighty movement of the Holy Ghost. Hinn has all the people close their eyes, until complete and total silence has swept the entire congregation. After a few moments, his microphone is turned up extremely loud, and he either begins blowing very loudly or yells, **"Take it!"** When this is done, everybody's autonomic nervous system is greatly jolted, and people begin falling down, thinking that the Holy Spirit has anointed them. It would basically be like sneaking up behind someone and screaming, "Boo!" There is nothing supernatural about how Benny "slays" people. As a matter of fact, it is all cheap illusion that completely plays on the emotions and natural reactions of people in a superpressurized situation.

Mr. Hinn is always coming up with some type of new revelation that keeps his listeners in utter amazement. He knows exactly how to entertain the excitement about the supernatural that dwells within all humanity. It is very difficult to understand how some of his foolish statements can ever be believable. It just goes to show you how undiscerning people are and how deceptive false prophets can be.

On April 21, 2000, Benny Hinn gave an absolutely outrageous story to his viewers on his daily *This Is*

Your Life program. The following foolishness will amaze you as to how anybody could believe this man's gobbledygook.

It is all cheap illusion that plays on the emotions and natural reactions of people.

You know one of these days we may show you what happened in our church in Orlando when I had the church in Florida. I was preaching, I was actually ministering on a Sunday night to the sick, when the people began screaming as the Lord's face appeared on the balcony. We have it on video. The Lord's face appeared on the balcony, and what was so remarkable is right before, the same face appeared in the children's church on a blackboard. And a little child sitting there with crippled legs was healed instantly. The teacher comes running down from the balcony screaming and shouting, the kids are all behind her, telling us how the Lord had appeared up there. And when she came running down, that's when the face of the Lord appeared in the main sanctuary. She was screaming, we all began screaming, and for eight weeks the Lord's face sat on that balcony, on the wall. And what was even more remarkable is that night, that Sunday night service when I was having a

> **healing service, as I was speaking the mouth was moving. The mouth—the Lord's face on the wall and you could see the mouth moving as I was speaking. And we thought—it was maybe, you know—it had to do with the lights, you know—just how we are all human beings, we're like Thomas, and sometimes we say, "Is this for real?" And—and—and the next day, Monday, the lights were all out—it was still there! Eight weeks later it was still there.**

My friend, if you have read this far and still hav the notion that Benny Hinn is a "man of God," the I believe you are very much under the delusion o the Devil. Jesus said, "The Spirit...will guide yo into all truth." That is not referring to the truth o man. Rather, it is speaking of the truth of the Wor of God. How could a born-again Christian read th Bible and still believe the outrageous and demoni statements that this false prophet has been makin for years?

8

THE TIP OF THE ICEBERG

We have merely touched the tip of the iceberg with regard to the "ministry" of Benny Hinn. He has made hundreds of these false and phony statements. On his daily television program, on TBN interviews and during his "Miracle Crusades," Mr. Hinn makes incredible, unbiblical statements. His sermons are full of this fairy tale nonsense that he attributes to the Holy Spirit. We have not even dealt with other aspects of deception and misrepresentation.

You should do a study on the way he throws **"FIRE!"** on those in his congregations. If you watch many of his videos, you will notice that he most always ends his prayer, **"In my Master's name. Amen."** By not using a name, he leaves open the question about who this master is. One thing is for sure: if you study the Bible, you will see that he is definitely not properly representing the God of the Bible.

As we bring this simple study to a close, notice what God Almighty says in His Word about false prophets:

"But there were false prophets also among the people, even as there shall be false teachers among you, who privily shall bring in damnable heresies, even denying the Lord that brought them and bring upon themselves swift destruction. And many shall follow their pernicious ways; by reason of whom the way of truth shall be evil spoken of. And through covetousness shall they with feigned words make merchandise of you: whose judgment now of a long time lingereth not, and their damnation slumbereth not."—II Pet. 2:1–3.

In conclusion, I must make this statement: *Benny Hinn is not the enemy, but I do believe he is doing the work of the enemy*. I do not hate Benny Hinn. I hate what he stands for and how the Devil has used him to lead millions astray. It is my prayer that this man will turn from his errors and will also be in Heaven for eternity.

Greg Locke
MINISTRIES

"The little man, with a great big God..."

Evangelist Greg Locke
212 Woodcraft Rd.
Murfreesboro, TN 37127

(615) 405–1665
(615) 896–0725

www.greglockeministries.com
or
www.greglocke.org

For a complete list of books available from the Sword of the Lord, write to Sword of the Lord Publishers, P. O. Box 1099, Murfreesboro, Tennessee 37133.

(800) 251-4100
(615) 893-6700
FAX (615) 848-6943
www.swordofthelord.com